The Visit

The Visit

Poems by

IAN HAMILTON

FABER AND FABER
London

First published in 1970
by Faber and Faber Limited
24 Russell Square London WC1
Reprinted 1970
Printed in Great Britain by
the Bowering Press Plymouth

SBN 571 09369 8

To Gisela

Acknowledgments

Some of these poems have appeared in the following periodicals: *Agenda*, the *London Magazine*, the *Listener*, the *New Statesman*, the *Observer*, the *Paris Review*, the *Times Literary Supplement*, the *Poetry Book Society Supplement* (Xmas 1962 and 1969), *P.E.N. New Poems 1967*.

Contents

The Storm

Miles off, a storm breaks. It ripples to our room.
You look up into the light so it catches one side
Of your face, your tight mouth, your startled eye.
You turn to me and when I call you come
Over and kneel beside me, wanting me to take
Your head between my hands as if it were
A delicate bowl that the storm might break.
You want me to get between you and the brute thunder.
But settling on your flesh my great hands stir,
Pulse on you and then, wondering how to do it, grip.
The storm rolls through me as your mouth opens.

Pretending Not To Sleep

The waiting rooms are full of 'characters'
Pretending not to sleep.
Your eyes are open
But you're far away,
At home, *am Rhein*, with mother and the cats.
Your hair grazes my wrist.
My cold hand surprises you.

The porters yawn against the slot-machines
And watch contentedly; they know I've lost.
The last train
Is simmering outside, and overhead
Steam flowers in the station rafters.
Soft flecks of soot begin to settle
On your suddenly outstretched palms.
Your mouth is dry, excited, going home;

The velvet curtains,
Father dead, the road up to the village,
Your hands tightening in the thick fur
Of your mother's Persian, your dreams
Moving through Belgium now, full of your trip.

Trucks

At four, a line of trucks. Their light
Slops in and spreads across the ceiling,
Gleams, and goes. Aching, you turn back
From the wall and your hands reach out
Over me. They are caught
In the last beam and, pale,
They fly there now. You're taking off, you say,
And won't be back.
                    Your shadows soar.
My hands, they can merely touch down
On your shoulders and wait. Very soon
The trucks will be gone. Bitter, you will turn
Back again. We will join our cold hands together.

The Recruits

'Nothing moves', you say, and stare across the lawn
At the trees, loafing in queues, their leaves rigid;
At the flowers, edgy, poised. You turn and cry:
'The sun is everywhere. There will be no breeze.'

Birds line the gutters, and from our window
We see cats file across five gardens
To the shade and stand there, tense and sullen,
Watching the sky. You cry again: 'They know.'

The dead flies pile up on the window sill.
You scoop them into heaps. You weep on them.
You shudder as the silence darkens, till
It's perfect night in you. And then you scream.

Windfalls

The windfalls ripen on the lawn,
The flies won't be disturbed.
They doze and glisten,
They wait for the fresh falls
To wipe them out. Like warts,
A pair of them sleep on your wrist.
Disabled, sleek, they have their fill.

Another wind prepares. It will shake apples
For these suicidal flies. It will restore
To lethargy your pale, disfigured hand.

Bequest

It is midwinter now and I am warm,
Bedridden, glad to be outlived.
My furniture
Surrounds me. I can reach my books.
And you, night after night
Until 'the end'
Will sit with me.

Between us
There are medicines, this pain
And these unfinished poems I bequeath you.
It must often be like this.

We darken gently as you count the days.
Your breath on mine
Monotonously warm.

Father, dying

Your fingers, wisps of blanket hair
Caught in their nails, extend to touch
The bedside roses flaking in the heat.
White petals fall.
                    Trapped on your hand
They darken, cling in sweat, then curl
Dry out and drop away.
                    Hour after hour
They trickle from the branch. At last
It's clean and, when you touch it, cold.
You lean forward to watch the thorns
Pluck on your skin white pools
That bleed as your fist tightens. 'My hand's
In flower', you say, 'My blood excites
This petal dross. I'll live.'

Birthday Poem

Tight in your hands,
Your Empire Exhibition shaving mug.
You keep it now
As a spittoon, its bloated doves
Its 1938
Stained by the droppings of your blood.
Tonight
Half-suffocated, cancerous,
Deceived
You bite against its gilded china mouth
And wait for an attack.

Metaphor

Your shadows blossom now about your bed
Discolouring
The last irritated facts.
Your oriental dressing gown;
Its golden butterflies, laced to their silken leaves,
Ache from the sudden darkness at your door.
You talk of butterflies, their luxuries, their skills
And their imprisonment.
You say,
'By these analogies we live.'

The sound of water trembles at the lip
Of this glass you are about to smash;
Your curtains flame like corrugated shields
Across these late September fields of snow
That are killing you.

Last Illness

Entranced, you turn again and over there
It is white also. Rectangular white lawns
For miles, white walls between them. Snow.
You close your eyes. The terrible changes.

White movements in one corner of your room.
Between your hands, the flowers of your quilt
Are stormed. Dark shadows smudge
Their faded, impossible colours
But do not settle.

You hear the ice take hold. Along the street
The yellowed drifts, cleansed by a minute's fall,
Wait to be fouled again. Your final breath
Is in the air, pure white, and moving fast.

Last Respects

Your breathing slightly disarrays
A single row of petals
As you lean over him. Your fingers,
In the air, above his face,
Are elegant, perplexed. They pause
At his cold mouth
But won't touch down; thin shadows drift
On candle smoke into his hair.
Your friendly touch
Brings down more petals:
A colourful panic.

Funeral

The tall weeds trail their hair
And spiral lazily
Up from their barnacled black roots
As if to touch
(Though hardly caring)
The light that polishes their quiet pool.

Beyond this damp, unpopular beach
The funeral cars
(Bathed in their own light)
Are gliding home now
And the first spray is breaking on my skin.

This tolerant breeze will not disturb us,
Father and son. The hotel is alight.

Epitaph

The scent of old roses and tobacco
Takes me back.
It's almost twenty years
Since I last saw you
And our half-hearted love affair goes on.

You left me this:
A hand, half-open, motionless
On a green counterpane.
Enough to build
A few melancholy poems on.

If I had touched you then
One of us might have survived.

Complaint

I've done what I could. My boys run wild now.
They seek their chances while their mother rots here.
And up the road, the man,
My one man, who touched me everywhere,
Falls to bits under the ground.

I am dumpy, obtuse, old and out of it.
At night, I can feel my hands prowl over me,
Lightly probing at my breasts, my knees,
The folds of my belly,
Now and then pressing and sometimes,
In their hunger, tearing me.
I live alone.

My boys run, leaving their mother as they would a stone
That rolls on in the playground after the bell has gone.
I gather dust and I could almost love the grave.
To have small beasts room in me would be something.
But here, at eight again, I watch the blossoms break
Beyond this gravel yard.
I know how to behave.

Night Walk

Above us now, the bridge
The dual carriageway,
And the new cars, their solemn music
Cool, expectant, happily pursued.
Tonight, your eyes half-closed, you want to lean
But patiently, upon my arm.

You want to sleep, imagining you see
Again thin-shadowed, anxious pools of light
Swarm quietly across this dark canal
And fade upon the weeds;
These soft horizons,
Softer than my touch.

Poem

Ah, listen now
Each breath more temperate, more kind
More close to death.
Sleep on
And listen to these words
Faintly, and with a tentative alarm,
Refuse to waken you.

Admission

The chapped lips of the uniformed night porter
Mumble horribly against the misted glass
Of our black ambulance.
Our plight
Inspires a single, soldierly, contemptuous stare
And then he waves us on, to Blighty.

Last Waltz

From where we sit, we can just about identify
The faces of these people we don't know:
A shadowed semi-circle
Ranged around the huge, donated television set
That dominates the ward.

The *Last Waltz* floods over them
Illuminating
Fond, exhausted smiles. And we,
As if we cared, are smiling too.

To each lost soul, at this late hour
A medicated pang of happiness.

Home

This weather won't let up. Above our heads
The houses lean upon each other's backs
And suffer the dark sleet that lashes them
Downhill. One window is alight.

'That's where I live.' My father's sleepless eye
Is burning down on us. The ice
That catches in your hair melts on my tongue.

Memorial

Four weathered gravestones tilt against the wall
Of your Victorian asylum.
Out of bounds, you kneel in the long grass
Deciphering obliterated names:
Old lunatics who died here.

The Visit

They've let me walk with you
As far as this high wall. The placid smiles
Of our new friends, the old incurables,
Pursue us lovingly.
Their boyish, suntanned heads
Their ancient arms
Outstretched, belong to you.

Although your head still burns
Your hands remember me.

The Vow

O world leave this alone
At least
This shocked and slightly aromatic fall of leaves
She gathers now and presses to her mouth
And swears on. Swears that love,
What's left of it,
Will sleep now, unappeased, impossible.

Your Cry

Your mouth, a thread of dying grass
Sealed to its lower lip,
At last is opening. We are alone,
You used to say,
And in each other's care.

Your cry
Has interrupted nothing and our hands,
Limp in each other's hair,
Have lost their touch.

Awakening

Your head, so sick, is leaning against mine,
So sensible. You can't remember
Why you're here, nor do you recognise
These helping hands.
My love,
The world encircles us. We're losing ground.

Aftermath

You eat out of my hand,
Exhausted animal. Your hair
Hangs from my wrist.

I promise that when your destruction comes
It will be mine
Who could have come between you.

Nature

I sit beneath this gleaming wall of rock
And let the breeze lap over me.
It's pleasant
Counting syllables in perfect scenery
Now that you're gone.

Words

You've had no life at all
To speak of, silent child.
Tonight
Your mother's German lullaby
Broke into tears
Upon your dreamless head
And you awoke in joy
To welcome her unanswerable cry.

Old Photograph

You are wandering in the deep field
That backs on to the room I used to work in
And from time to time
You look up to see if I am watching you.
To this day
Your arms are full of the wild flowers
You were most in love with.

Neighbours

From the bay windows
Of the mouldering hotel across the road from us
Mysterious, one-night itinerants emerge
On to their balconies
To breathe the cool night air.

We let them stare
In at our quiet lives.
They let us wonder what's become of them.

Breaking Up

He's driving now,
The father of your family,
Somewhere up north. Before he left
You shared out your three hundred books
Together. He has taken those you've read
And left behind
Those you have secretly decided
Are unreadable.

Newscast

The Vietnam war drags on
In one corner of our living room.
The conversation turns
To take it in.
Our smoking heads
Drift back to us
From the grey fires of South East Asia.

Curfew

It's midnight
And our silent house is listening
To the last sounds of people going home.
We lie beside our curtained window
Wondering
What makes them do it.

Now and Then

The white walls of the Institution
Overlook a strip of thriving meadowland.
On clear days, we can walk there
And look back upon your 'second home'
From the green shelter
Of this wild, top-heavy tree.

It all seems so long ago. This afternoon
A gentle sun
Smiles on the tidy avenues, the lawns,
The miniature allotments,
On the barred windows of the brand new
Chronic block, 'our pride and joy'.
At the main gate
Pale visitors are hurrying from cars.

It all seems so far away. This afternoon
The smoke from our abandoned cigarettes
Climbs in a single column to the sky.
A gentle sun
Smiles on the dark, afflicted heads
Of young men who have come to nothing.